Cram101 Textbook Outlines to accompany:

Strategic Management & Business Policy: Achieving Sustainability

Thomas L. Wheelen, 12th Edition

A Cram101 Inc. publication (c) 2010.

Cram101 Textbook Outlines and Cram101.com are Cram101 Inc. publications and services. All notes, highlights, reviews, and practice tests are written and prepared by Cram101, all rights reserved.

PRACTICE EXAMS.

Get all of the self-teaching practice exams for each chapter of this textbook at **www.Cram101.com** and ace the tests. Here is an example:

Chapter 1

Strategic Management & Business Policy: Achieving Sustainability
Thomas L. Wheelen, 12th Edition,
All Material Written and Prepared by Cram101

I WANT A BETTER GRADE. Items 1 - 50 of 100.

1. _____ is a business management strategy, initially implemented by Motorola, that today enjoys widespread application in many sectors of industry.

   _____ seeks to improve the quality of process outputs by identifying and removing the causes of defects (errors) and variation in manufacturing and business processes. It uses a set of quality management methods, including statistical methods, and creates a special infrastructure of people within the organization ('Black Belts' etc.)

   - Six Sigma
   - S corporation
   - SA8000
   - Sabbath

2. A _____ is a legally recognized organization designed to provide goods and/or services to consumers. _____ es are predominant in capitalist economies, most being privately owned and formed to earn profit that will increase the wealth of its owners and grow the _____ itself. The owners and operators of a _____ have as one of their main objectives the receipt or generation of a financial return in exchange for work and acceptance of risk.

   - Business
   - B2C
   - Back office
   - Backdating

3. A _____ is typically described as a deliberate plan of action to guide decisions and achieve rational outcome(s). However, the term may also be used to denote what is actually done, even though it is unplanned.

You get a 50% discount for the online exams. Go to **Cram101.com**, click Sign Up at the top of the screen, and enter DK73DW8101 in the promo code box on the registration screen. Access to Cram101.com is $4.95 per month, cancel at any time.

With Cram101.com online, you also have access to extensive reference material.

You will nail those essays and papers. Here is an example from a Cram101 Biology text:

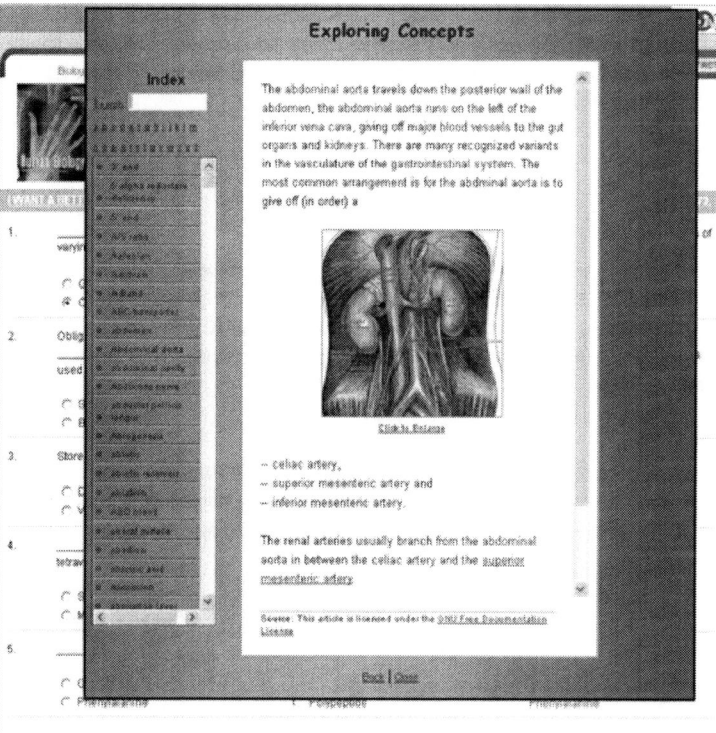

Visit **www.Cram101.com**, click Sign Up at the top of the screen, and enter DK73DW8101 in the promo code box on the registration screen. Access to www.Cram101.com is normally $9.95 per month, but because you have purchased this book, your access fee is only $4.95 per month, cancel at any time. Sign up and stop highlighting textbooks forever.

Learning System

Cram101 Textbook Outlines is a learning system. The notes in this book are the highlights of your textbook, you will never have to highlight a book again.

How to use this book. Take this book to class, it is your notebook for the lecture. The notes and highlights on the left hand side of the pages follow the outline and order of the textbook. All you have to do is follow along while your instructor presents the lecture. Circle the items emphasized in class and add other important information on the right side. With Cram101 Textbook Outlines you'll spend less time writing and more time listening. Learning becomes more efficient.

Cram101.com Online

Increase your studying efficiency by using Cram101.com's practice tests and online reference material. It is the perfect complement to Cram101 Textbook Outlines. Use self-teaching matching tests or simulate in-class testing with comprehensive multiple choice tests, or simply use Cram's true and false tests for quick review. Cram101.com even allows you to enter your in-class notes for an integrated studying format combining the textbook notes with your class notes.

Visit **www.Cram101.com**, click Sign Up at the top of the screen, and enter **DK73DW8101** in the promo code box on the registration screen. Access to www.Cram101.com is normally $9.95 per month, but because you have purchased this book, your access fee is only $4.95 per month. Sign up and stop highlighting textbooks forever.

Copyright © 2010 by Cram101, Inc. All rights reserved. "Cram101"® and "Never Highlight a Book Again!"® are registered trademarks of Cram101, Inc. ISBN(s): 9781428890176.

Strategic Management & Business Policy: Achieving Sustainability
Thomas L. Wheelen, 12th

CONTENTS

1. Basic Concepts of Strategic Management 2
2. Corporate Governance 10
3. Social Responsibility and Ethics in Strategic Management 16
4. Environmental Scanning and Industry Analysis 18
5. Internal Scanning: Organizational Analysis 26
6. Strategy Formulation: Situation Analysis and Business Strategy 38
7. Strategy Formulation: Corporate Strategy 44
8. Strategy Formulation: Functional Strategy and Strategic Choice 50
9. Strategy Implementation: Organizing for Action 60
10. Strategy Implementation: Staffing and Directing 68
11. Evaluation and Control 74
12. Suggestions for Case Analysis 86

Chapter 1. Basic Concepts of Strategic Management

Six Sigma	Six Sigma is a business management strategy, initially implemented by Motorola, that today enjoys widespread application in many sectors of industry.
	Six Sigma seeks to improve the quality of process outputs by identifying and removing the causes of defects (errors) and variation in manufacturing and business processes. It uses a set of quality management methods, including statistical methods, and creates a special infrastructure of people within the organization ('Black Belts' etc.)
Business	A Business is a legally recognized organization designed to provide goods and/or services to consumers. Business es are predominant in capitalist economies, most being privately owned and formed to earn profit that will increase the wealth of its owners and grow the Business itself. The owners and operators of a Business have as one of their main objectives the receipt or generation of a financial return in exchange for work and acceptance of risk.
Policy	A Policy is typically described as a deliberate plan of action to guide decisions and achieve rational outcome(s.) However, the term may also be used to denote what is actually done, even though it is unplanned.
	The term may apply to government, private sector organizations and groups, and individuals.
Globalization	Globalization in its literal sense is the process of transformation of local or regional phenomena into global ones. It can be described as a process by which the people of the world are unified into a single society and function together.
	This process is a combination of economic, technological, sociocultural and political forces.
Industry trade group	An industry trade group is an organization founded and funded by businesses that operate in a specific industry. An industry trade association participates in public relations activities such as advertising, education, political donations, lobbying and publishing, but its main focus is collaboration between companies, or standardization. Associations may offer other services, such as producing conferences, networking or charitable events or offering classes or educational materials.
Learning organization	A Learning organization is the term given to a company that facilitates the learning of its members and continuously transforms itself. Learning organization s develop as a result of the pressures facing modern organizations and enables them to remain competitive in the business environment. A Learning organization has five main features; systems thinking, personal mastery, mental models, shared vision and team learning.
Organizational learning	Organizational learning is an area of knowledge within organizational theory that studies models and theories about the way an organization learns and adapts.
	In Organizational development (OD), learning is a characteristic of an adaptive organization, i.e., an organization that is able to sense changes in signals from its environment (both internal and external) and adapt accordingly.
Choice	Choice consists of the mental process of thinking involved with the process of judging the merits of multiple options and selecting one of them for action. Some simple examples include deciding whether to get up in the morning or go back to sleep, or selecting a given route for a journey. More complex examples (often decisions that affect what a person thinks or their core beliefs) include choosing a lifestyle, religious affiliation, or political position.
Management process	Management process is a process of planning and controlling the performance or execution of any type of activity, such as:

Chapter 1. Basic Concepts of Strategic Management

Chapter 1. Basic Concepts of Strategic Management

· a project (project Management process) or
· a process (process Management process, sometimes referred to as the process performance measurement and management system.)

Organization's senior management is responsible for carrying out its Management process.

Environmental scanning

Environmental scanning is a process of gathering, analyzing, and dispensing information for tactical or strategic purposes. The Environmental scanning process entails obtaining both factual and subjective information on the business environments in which a company is operating or considering entering.

There are three ways of scanning the business environment:

· Ad-hoc scanning - Short term, infrequent examinations usually initiated by a crisis
· Regular scanning - Studies done on a regular schedule (say, once a year)
· Continuous scanning(also called continuous learning) - continuous structured data collection and processing on a broad range of environmental factors

Most commentators feel that in today's turbulent business environment the best scanning method available is continuous scanning. This allows the firm to :

-act quickly-take advantage of opportunities before competitors do-respond to environmental threats before significant damage is done

SWOT analysis

SWOT analysis is a strategic planning method used to evaluate the Strengths, Weaknesses, Opportunities, and Threats involved in a project or in a business venture. It involves specifying the objective of the business venture or project and identifying the internal and external factors that are favorable and unfavorable to achieving that objective. The technique is credited to Albert Humphrey, who led a convention at Stanford University in the 1960s and 1970s using data from Fortune 500 companies.

Mission statement

A mission statement is a brief written statement of the purpose of a company or organization. Ideally, a mission statement guides the actions of the organization, spells out its overall goal, provides a sense of direction, and guides decision making for all levels of management.

mission statement s often contain the following:

· Purpose and aim of the organization
· The organization's primary stakeholders: clients, stockholders, etc.
· Responsibilities of the organization toward these stakeholders
· Products and services offered

In developing a mission statement

· Encourage as much input as feasible from employees, volunteers, and other stakeholders
· Publicize it broadly
· Limit to a few statements.

The mission statement can be used to resolve differences between business stakeholders.

Chapter 1. Basic Concepts of Strategic Management

Goal	A Goal or objective is a projected state of affairs that a person or a system plans or intends to achieve--a personal or organizational desired end-point in some sort of assumed development. Many people endeavor to reach Goal s within a finite time by setting deadlines. A desire or an intention becomes a Goal if and only if one activates an action for achieving it
Business strategy	Business strategy refers to the aggregated strategies of single business firm or a strategic business unit (SBU) in a diversified corporation. According to Michael Porter, a firm must formulate a Business strategy that incorporates either cost leadership, differentiation or focus in order to achieve a sustainable competitive advantage and long-term success in its chosen arenas or industries. Functional strategies include marketing strategies, new product development strategies, human resource strategies, financial strategies, legal strategies, supply-chain strategies, and information technology management strategies.
Corporate strategy	Corporate strategy refers to the overarching strategy of the diversified firm. Such a Corporate strategy answers the questions of 'in which businesses should we be in?' and 'how does being in these business create synergy and/or add to the competitive advantage of the corporation as a whole?' Business strategy refers to the aggregated strategies of single business firm or a strategic business unit (SBU) in a diversified corporation. According to Michael Porter, a firm must formulate a business strategy that incorporates either cost leadership, differentiation or focus in order to achieve a sustainable competitive advantage and long-term success in its chosen arenas or industries.
Implementation	Implementation is the realization of an application idea, model, design, specification, standard, algorithm an Implementation is a realization of a technical specification or algorithm as a program, software component, or other computer system. Many Implementation s may exist for a given specification or standard.
Operational planning	An Operational planning is a subset of strategic work plan. It describes short-term ways of achieving milestones and explains how, or what portion of, a strategic plan will be put into operation during a given operational period, in the case of commercial application, a fiscal year or another given budgetary term. An operational plan is the basis for, and justification of an annual operating budget request.
Decision making	Decision making can be regarded as an outcome of mental processes (cognitive process) leading to the selection of a course of action among several alternatives. Every Decision making process produces a final choice. The output can be an action or an opinion of choice.
Budget	Budget generally refers to a list of all planned expenses and revenues. It is a plan for saving and spending. A Budget is an important concept in microeconomics, which uses a Budget line to illustrate the trade-offs between two or more goods.
Standard Operating Procedure	A Standard operating procedure is a set of instructions having the force of a directive, covering those features of operations that lend themselves to a definite or standardized procedure without loss of effectiveness. Standard Operating Policies and Procedures can be effective catalysts to drive performance improvement and improving organizational results.

Chapter 1. Basic Concepts of Strategic Management

Chapter 1. Basic Concepts of Strategic Management

Control	Control is one of the managerial functions like planning, organizing, staffing and directing. It is an important function because it helps to check the errors and to take the corrective action so that deviation from standards are minimized and stated goals of the organization are achieved in desired manner. According to modern concepts, Control is a foreseeing action whereas earlier concept of Control was used only when errors were detected. Control in management means setting standards, measuring actual performance and taking corrective action.
Cash cow	In business, a Cash cow is a product or a business unit that generates unusually high profit margins: so high that it is responsible for a large amount of a company's operating profit. This profit far exceeds the amount necessary to maintain the Cash cow business, and the excess is used by the business for other purposes. A firm is said to be acting as a Cash cow when its earnings per share (EPS) is equal to its dividends per share (DPS), or in other words, when a firm pays out 100% of its free cash flow (FCF) to its shareholders as dividends at the end of each accounting term.
Punctuated equilibrium	Punctuated Equilibrium is a theory in evolutionary biology which states that most sexually reproducing species will experience little evolutionary change for most of their geological history (in an extended state called stasis.) When evolution occurs, it is localized in rare, rapid events of branching speciation (called cladogenesis.) Cladogenesis is simply the process by which species split into two distinct species, rather than one species gradually transforming into another.
Incrementalism	Incrementalism is a method of working by adding to a project using many small (often unplanned) changes instead of a few (extensively planned) large jumps. Wikipedia, for example, illustrates the concept by building an encyclopedia bit by bit, continually adding to it. In a similar vein, it is said that Virgil wrote the Aeneid in an incremental process, averaging one line per day.
Audit	The general definition of an audit is an evaluation of a person, organization, system, process, project or product. audit s are performed to ascertain the validity and reliability of information; also to provide an assessment of a system's internal control. The goal of an audit is to express an opinion on the person / organization/system (etc) in question, under evaluation based on work done on a test basis.

Chapter 2. Corporate Governance

Board of directors	A Board of directors is a body of elected or appointed members who jointly oversee the activities of a company or organization. The body sometimes has a different name, such as board of trustees, board of governors, board of managers, or executive board. It is often simply referred to as 'the board.' A board's activities are determined by the powers, duties, and responsibilities delegated to it or conferred on it by an authority outside itself.
Corporate governance	Corporate governance is the set of processes, customs, policies, laws, and institutions affecting the way a corporation (or company) is directed, administered or controlled. Corporate governance also includes the relationships among the many stakeholders involved and the goals for which the corporation is governed. The principal stakeholders are the shareholders/members, management, and the board of directors.
Shareholder	A mutual Shareholder or stockholder is an individual or company (including a corporation) that legally owns one or more shares of stock in a joint stock company. A company's Shareholder s collectively own that company. Thus, the typical goal of such companies is to enhance Shareholder value.
Chief brand officer	A Chief brand officer is a relatively new executive level position at a corporation, company, organization typically reporting directly to the CEO or board of directors. The Chief brand officer is responsible for a brand's image, experience, and promise, and propagating it throughout all aspects of the company. The brand officer oversees marketing, advertising, design, public relations and customer service departments.
Principal-agent problem	In political science and economics, the principal-agent problem or agency dilemma treats the difficulties that arise under conditions of incomplete and asymmetric information when a principal hires an agent, such as the problem that the two may not have the same interests, while the principal is, presumably, hiring the agent to pursue the interests of the former. Various mechanisms may be used to try to align the interests of the agent with those of the principal, such as piece rates/commissions, profit sharing, efficiency wages, performance measurement (including financial statements), the agent posting a bond, or fear of firing. The principal-agent problem is found in most employer/employee relationships, for example, when stockholders hire top executives of corporations.
Inside director	An Inside director is a member of the Board of Directors of a corporation who is also a member of the corporation's management, almost always a corporate officer. For example, a Chief Executive Officer who is also Chairman of the Board would be considered an Inside director. A Chief Financial Officer, Executive Vice President, or other corporate executive who is a member of the board is also an Inside director.
Numerary	Numerary is a civil designation for persons who are incorporated in a fixed or permanent way to a society or group: regular member of the working staff, permanent staff distinguished from a super Numerary . The term Numerary and its counterpart, 'super Numerary ,' originated in Spanish and Latin American academy and government; it is now also used in countries all over the world, such as France, the U.S., England, Italy, etc. There are Numerary members of surgical organizations, of universities, of gastronomical associations, etc.
Co-determination	Co-determination is a practice whereby the employees have a role in management of a company. The word is a somewhat clumsy and literal translation from the German word Mitbestimmung. Co-determination rights are different in different legal environments.

Chapter 2. Corporate Governance

Chapter 2. Corporate Governance

Interlocking directorate	Interlocking directorate refers to the practice of members of corporate board of directors serving on the boards of multiple corporations. This practice, although widespread and lawful, raises questions about the quality and independence of board decisions. The average board of directors has nine members, and the total population of board members of public companies traded on the NYSE, NASDAQ and AMEX stock exchanges is about 53,000.
Keiretsu	A Keiretsu is a set of companies with interlocking business relationships and shareholdings. It is a type of business group. The prototypical Keiretsu are those which appeared in Japan during the 'economic miracle' following World War II.
Sarbanes-Oxley Act	The Sarbanes-Oxley Act of 2002 (Pub.L. 107-204, 116 Stat. 745, enacted July 30, 2002), also known as the Public Company Accounting Reform and Investor Protection Act of 2002 and commonly called Sarbanes-Oxley, Sarbox or SOX, is a United States federal law enacted on July 30, 2002, as a reaction to a number of major corporate and accounting scandals including those affecting Enron, Tyco International, Adelphia, Peregrine Systems and WorldCom.
Whistleblower	A Whistleblower is a person who alleges misconduct. More complex definitions may be used, but the issue is that the Whistleblower usually faces reprisal. The misconduct may be classified in many ways; for example, a violation of a law, rule, regulation and/or a direct threat to public interest, such as fraud, health/safety violations, and corruption.
Institutional investors	Institutional investors are organizations which pool large sums of money and invest those sums in companies. They include banks, insurance companies, retirement or pension funds, hedge funds and mutual funds. Their role in the economy is to act as highly specialized investors on behalf of others.
Investor	An Investor is any party that makes an investment. The term has taken on a specific meaning in finance to describe the particular types of people and companies that regularly purchase equity or debt securities for financial gain in exchange for funding an expanding company. Less frequently, the term is applied to parties who purchase real estate, currency, commodity derivatives, personal property, or other assets.
Trend analysis	The term 'Trend analysis' refers to the concept of collecting information and attempting to spot a pattern in the information. In some fields of study, the term 'Trend analysis' has more formally-defined meanings. In project management Trend analysis is a mathematical technique that uses historical results to predict future outcome.
Leadership	Leadership has been described as the 'process of social influence in which one person can enlist the aid and support of others in the accomplishment of a common task' . A definition more inclusive of followers comes from Alan Keith of Genentech who said 'leadership is ultimately about creating a way for people to contribute to making something extraordinary happen.' leadership is one of the most salient aspects of the organizational context. However, defining leadership has been challenging.

Chapter 2. Corporate Governance

Chapter 2. Corporate Governance

Strategic planning	Strategic planning is an organization's process of defining its strategy and making decisions on allocating its resources to pursue this strategy, including its capital and people. Various business analysis techniques can be used in Strategic planning, including SWOT analysis (Strengths, Weaknesses, Opportunities, and Threats) and PEST analysis (Political, Economic, Social, and Technological analysis) or STEER analysis involving Socio-cultural, Technological, Economic, Ecological, and Regulatory factors and EPISTEL (Environment, Political, Informatic, Social, Technological, Economic and Legal) Strategic planning is the formal consideration of an organization's future course. All Strategic planning deals with at least one of three key questions: · 'What do we do?' · 'For whom do we do it?' · 'How do we excel?' In business Strategic planning, the third question is better phrased 'How can we beat or avoid competition?'. (Bradford and Duncan, page 1.)
Chief Strategy Officer	A Chief strategy officer is an executive who is responsible for assisting the chief executive officer with creating, communicating, executing, and sustaining strategic initiatives within a corporation. A typical Chief strategy officer is not a pure strategist that creates long-term planning that is isolated from the corporation's current initiatives. Many Chief strategy officer s are considered 'doers' first and have the past experience to help advise and execute.

Chapter 3. Social Responsibility and Ethics in Strategic Management

Laissez-faire	Laissez-faire is a term used to describe a policy of allowing events to take their own course. The term is a French phrase literally meaning 'let do'. It is a doctrine that states that government generally should not intervene in the marketplace.
Business	A Business is a legally recognized organization designed to provide goods and/or services to consumers. Business es are predominant in capitalist economies, most being privately owned and formed to earn profit that will increase the wealth of its owners and grow the Business itself. The owners and operators of a Business have as one of their main objectives the receipt or generation of a financial return in exchange for work and acceptance of risk.
Stakeholder analysis	Stakeholder analysis is a term used in project management and business administration to describe a process where all the individuals or groups that are likely to be affected by the activities of a project are identified and then sorted according to how much they can affect the project and how much the project can affect them. This information is used to assess how the interests of those stakeholders should be addressed in the project plan. A stakeholder is any person or organization, who can be positively or negatively impacted by, or cause an impact on the actions of a company.
Business ethics	Business ethics is a form of applied ethics that examines ethical principles and moral or ethical problems that arise in a business environment. It applies to all aspects of business conduct and is relevant to the conduct of individuals and business organizations as a whole. Applied ethics is a field of ethics that deals with ethical questions in many fields such as medical, technical, legal and Business ethics.
Decision making	Decision making can be regarded as an outcome of mental processes (cognitive process) leading to the selection of a course of action among several alternatives. Every Decision making process produces a final choice. The output can be an action or an opinion of choice.
Capitalism	Capitalism is an economic and social system in which trade and industry are privately controlled for profit. The means of production, which is otherwise known as capital and includes land are owned, operated, and traded for the purpose of generating profits, without force or fraud, by private individuals either singly or jointly. Investments, distribution, income, production, pricing and supply of goods, commodities and services are determined by voluntary private decision in Capitalism, which is also known as a market economy.
Moral relativism	In philosophy moral relativism is the position that moral or ethical propositions do not reflect objective and/or universal moral truths, but instead make claims relative to social, cultural, historical or personal circumstances. Moral relativists hold that no universal standard exists by which to assess an ethical proposition's truth. Relativistic positions often see moral values as applicable only within certain cultural boundaries (cultural relativism) or in the context of individual preferences (individualist ethical subjectivism.)
Whistleblower	A Whistleblower is a person who alleges misconduct. More complex definitions may be used, but the issue is that the Whistleblower usually faces reprisal. The misconduct may be classified in many ways; for example, a violation of a law, rule, regulation and/or a direct threat to public interest, such as fraud, health/safety violations, and corruption.

Chapter 4. Environmental Scanning and Industry Analysis

Environmental scanning	Environmental scanning is a process of gathering, analyzing, and dispensing information for tactical or strategic purposes. The Environmental scanning process entails obtaining both factual and subjective information on the business environments in which a company is operating or considering entering.
	There are three ways of scanning the business environment:
	· Ad-hoc scanning - Short term, infrequent examinations usually initiated by a crisis
	· Regular scanning - Studies done on a regular schedule (say, once a year)
	· Continuous scanning(also called continuous learning) - continuous structured data collection and processing on a broad range of environmental factors
	Most commentators feel that in today's turbulent business environment the best scanning method available is continuous scanning. This allows the firm to :
	-act quickly-take advantage of opportunities before competitors do-respond to environmental threats before significant damage is done
Externalities	Many negative Externalities are related to the environmental consequences of production and use
	· Systemic risk describes the risks to the overall economy arising from the risks which the banking system takes. That the private costs of banking failure may be smaller than the social costs justifies banking regulations, although regulations could create a moral hazard.
	· Anthropogenic climate change is attributed to greenhouse gas emissions from burning oil, gas, and coal. Global warming has been ranked as the #1 externality of all economic activity, in the magnitude of potential harms and yet remains unmitigated.
Multinational Corporation	A Multinational corporation or transnational corporation is a corporation or enterprise that manages production or delivers services in more than one country. It can also be referred to as an international corporation.
	The first modern Multinational corporation is generally thought to be the Dutch East India Company, established in 1602.
Purchasing power	Purchasing power is the number of goods/services that can be purchased with a unit of currency. For example, if you had taken one dollar to a store in the 1950s, you would have been able to buy a greater number of items than you would today, indicating that you would have had a greater Purchasing power in the 1950s. Currency can be either a commodity money, like gold or silver, or fiat currency like US dollars.
Purchasing power parity	The Purchasing power parity theory uses the long-term equilibrium exchange rate of two currencies to equalize their purchasing power. Developed by Gustav Cassel in 1918, it is based on the law of one price: the theory states that, in ideally efficient markets, identical goods should have only one price.
	This purchasing power SEM rate equalizes the purchasing power of different currencies in their home countries for a given basket of goods.

Chapter 4. Environmental Scanning and Industry Analysis

Cost	In economics, business, retail, and accounting, a Cost is the value of money that has been used up to produce something, and hence is not available for use anymore. In economics, a Cost is an alternative that is given up as a result of a decision. In business, the Cost may be one of acquisition, in which case the amount of money expended to acquire it is counted as Cost.
Transaction cost	In economics and related disciplines, a Transaction cost is a cost incurred in making an economic exchange (restated: the cost of participating in a market.) For example, most people, when buying or selling a stock, must pay a commission to their broker; that commission is a Transaction cost of doing the stock deal. Or consider buying a banana from a store; to purchase the banana, your costs will be not only the price of the banana itself, but also the energy and effort it requires to find out which of the various banana products you prefer, where to get them and at what price, the cost of traveling from your house to the store and back, the time waiting in line, and the effort of the paying itself; the costs above and beyond the cost of the banana are the Transaction cost s.
Switching cost	Switching barriers or Switching cost s are terms used in microeconomics, strategic management, and marketing to describe any impediment to a customer's changing of suppliers. In many markets, consumers are forced to incur costs when switching from one supplier to another. These costs are called Switching cost s and can come in many different shapes.
Job interview	A Job interview is a process in which a potential employee is evaluated by an employer for prospective employment in their company, organization and was established in the late 16th century. A Job interview typically precedes the hiring decision, and is used to evaluate the candidate. The interview is usually preceded by the evaluation of submitted résumés from interested candidates, then selecting a small number of candidates for interviews.
Bargaining power	Bargaining power is a concept related to the relative abilities of parties in a situation to exert influence over each other. If both parties are on an equal footing in a debate, then they will have equal Bargaining power, such as in a perfectly competitive market, or between an evenly matched monopoly and monopsony. There are a number of fields where the concept of Bargaining power has proven crucial to coherent analysis: game theory, labour economics, collective bargaining arrangements, diplomatic negotiations, settlement of litigation, the price of insurance, and any negotiation in general.
Commodity	A Commodity is something for which there is demand, but which is supplied without qualitative differentiation across a market. It is a product that is the same no matter who produces it, such as petroleum, notebook paper, or milk. In other words, copper is copper.
Barriers to exit	In economics, barriers to exit are obstacles in the path of a firm which wants to leave a given market or industrial sector. These obstacles often cost the firm financially to leave the market and may prohibit it doing so. If the barriers of exit are significant; a firm may be forced to continue competing in a market, as the costs of leaving may be higher than those incurred if they continue competing in the market.

Chapter 4. Environmental Scanning and Industry Analysis

Chapter 4. Environmental Scanning and Industry Analysis

Strategic group	A Strategic group is a concept used in strategic management that groups companies within an industry that have similar business models or similar combinations of strategies. For example, the restaurant industry can be divided into several Strategic group s including fast-food and fine-dining based on variables such as preparation time, pricing, and presentation. The number of groups within an industry and their composition depends on the dimensions used to define the groups.
Hypercompetition	Often a characteristic of new markets and industries, Hypercompetition occurs when technologies or offerings are so new that standards and rules are in flux, resulting in competitive advantages that cannot be sustained. In response, companies must constantly compete in price or quality, or innovate in supply chain management, new value creation, or have enough financial capital to outlast other competitors.
Business	A Business is a legally recognized organization designed to provide goods and/or services to consumers. Business es are predominant in capitalist economies, most being privately owned and formed to earn profit that will increase the wealth of its owners and grow the Business itself. The owners and operators of a Business have as one of their main objectives the receipt or generation of a financial return in exchange for work and acceptance of risk.
Competitive intelligence	A broad definition of Competitive intelligence is the action of gathering, analyzing, and distributing information about products, customers, competitors and any aspect of the environment needed to support executives and managers in making strategic decisions for an organization. Key points of this definitions: · Competitive intelligence is an ethical and legal business practice. (This is important as Competitive intelligence professionals emphasize that the discipline is not the same as industrial espionage which is both unethical and usually illegal.) · The focus is on the external business environment. · There is a process involved in gathering information, converting it into intelligence and then utilizing this in business decision making. Competitive intelligence professionals emphasize that if the intelligence gathered is not usable (or actionable) then it is not intelligence. A more focused definition of Competitive intelligence regards it as the organizational function responsible for the early identification of risks and opportunities in the market before they become obvious. Experts also call this process the early signal analysis. This definition focuses attention on the difference between dissemination of widely available factual information (such as market statistics, financial reports, newspaper clippings) performed by functions such as libraries and information centers, and Competitive intelligence which is a perspective on developments and events aimed at yielding a competitive edge.
Forecasting	Forecasting is the process of estimation in unknown situations. Prediction is a similar, but more general term. Both can refer to estimation of time series, cross-sectional or longitudinal data.
Brainstorming	Brainstorming is a group creativity technique designed to generate a large number of ideas for the solution of a problem. The method was first popularized in the late 1930s by Alex Faickney Osborn in a book called Applied Imagination. Osborn proposed that groups could double their creative output with Brainstorming.

Chapter 4. Environmental Scanning and Industry Analysis

Chapter 4. Environmental Scanning and Industry Analysis

Delphi method	The Delphi method is a systematic, interactive forecasting method which relies on a panel of independent experts. The carefully selected experts answer questionnaires in two or more rounds. After each round, a facilitator provides an anonymous summary of the experts' forecasts from the previous round as well as the reasons they provided for their judgments.
Statistical model	A statistical model is a set of mathematical equations which describe the behavior of an object of study in terms of random variables and their associated probability distributions. If the model has only one equation it is called a single-equation model, whereas if it has more than one equation, it is known as a multiple-equation model. In mathematical terms, a statistical model is frequently thought of as a pair (Y,P) where Y is the set of possible observations and P the set of possible probability distributions on Y.
Market	A market is any one of a variety of different systems, institutions, procedures, social relations and infrastructures whereby persons trade, and goods and services are exchanged, forming part of the economy. It is an arrangement that allows buyers and sellers to exchange things. market s vary in size, range, geographic scale, location, types and variety of human communities, as well as the types of goods and services traded.
Audit	The general definition of an audit is an evaluation of a person, organization, system, process, project or product. audit s are performed to ascertain the validity and reliability of information; also to provide an assessment of a system's internal control. The goal of an audit is to express an opinion on the person / organization/system (etc) in question, under evaluation based on work done on a test basis.
Game	A Game is a structured activity, usually undertaken for enjoyment and sometimes used as an educational tool. Game s are distinct from work, which is usually carried out for remuneration, and from art, which is more concerned with the expression of ideas. However, the distinction is not clear-cut, and many Game s are also considered to be work (such as professional players of spectator sports/ Game s) or art (such as jigsaw puzzles or Game s involving an artistic layout such as Mah-jongg solitaire.)

Chapter 4. Environmental Scanning and Industry Analysis

Chapter 5. Internal Scanning: Organizational Analysis

Asset	In business and accounting, asset s are economic resources owned by business or company. Anything tangible or intangible that one possesses, usually considered as applicable to the payment of one's debts is considered an asset Simplistically stated, asset s are things of value that can be readily converted into cash.
Core competency	Core competency is something that a firm can do well and that meets the following three conditions:
	Competencies are things that companys execute well across several business units or product sectors.
	Firms usually have few competencies, but these are usually less liable to change rapidly.
	· It provides consumer benefits · It is not easy for competitors to imitate · It can be leveraged widely to many products and markets. A Core competency can take various forms, including technical/subject matter know-how, a reliable process and/or close relationships with customers and suppliers (Mascarenhas et al. 1998.)
Intangible assets	Intangible assets are defined as identifiable non-monetary assets that cannot be seen, touched or physically measured, which are created through time and/or effort and that are identifiable as a separate asset. There are two primary forms of intangibles - legal intangibles (such as trade secrets (e.g., customer lists), copyrights, patents, trademarks, and goodwill) and competitive intangibles (such as knowledge activities (know-how, knowledge), collaboration activities, leverage activities, and structural activities.) Legal intangibles are known under the generic term intellectual property and generate legal property rights defensible in a court of law.
Competitive advantage	Competitive advantage is, in very basic words, a position a firm occupies against its competitors.
	According to Michael Porter, the three methods for creating a sustainable Competitive advantage are through: 1. Cost leadership 2. Differentiation 3. Focus (economics)
Reverse engineering	Reverse engineering is the process of discovering the technological principles of a device, object or system through analysis of its structure, function and operation. It often involves taking something (e.g., a mechanical device, electronic component, or software program) apart and analyzing its workings in detail to be used in maintenance, or to try to make a new device or program that does the same thing without copying anything from the original.
	Reverse engineering has its origins in the analysis of hardware for commercial or military advantage .
Business	A Business is a legally recognized organization designed to provide goods and/or services to consumers. Business es are predominant in capitalist economies, most being privately owned and formed to earn profit that will increase the wealth of its owners and grow the Business itself. The owners and operators of a Business have as one of their main objectives the receipt or generation of a financial return in exchange for work and acceptance of risk.
Business model	A Business model is a framework for creating economic, social, and/or other forms of value. The term Business model is thus used for a broad range of informal and formal descriptions to represent core aspects of a business, including purpose, offerings, strategies, infrastructure, organizational structures, trading practices, and operational processes and policies.

Chapter 5. Internal Scanning: Organizational Analysis

	Conceptualization of Business model s try to formalize informal descriptions into building blocks and their relationships.
Value chain	The Value chain is a concept from business management that was first described and popularized by Michael Porter in his 1985 best-seller, Competitive Advantage: Creating and Sustaining Superior Performance.
	A Value chain is a chain of activities. Products pass through all activities of the chain in order and at each activity the product gains some value. The chain of activities gives the products more added value than the sum of added values of all activities. It is important not to mix the concept of the Value chain with the costs occurring throughout the activities.
Vertical integration	In microeconomics and management, the term vertical integration describes a style of management control. Vertically integrated companies are united through a hierarchy with a common owner. Usually each member of the hierarchy produces a different product or (market-specific) service, and the products combine to satisfy a common need.
Economies of scope	Economies of scope are conceptually similar to economies of scale. Whereas economies of scale primarily refer to efficiencies associated with supply-side changes, such as increasing or decreasing the scale of production, of a single product type, Economies of scope refer to efficiencies primarily associated with demand-side changes, such as increasing or decreasing the scope of marketing and distribution, of different types of products. Economies of scope are one of the main reasons for such marketing strategies as product bundling, product lining, and family branding.
Organizational structure	An Organizational structure is a mostly hierarchical concept of subordination of entities that collaborate and contribute to serve one common aim.
	Organizations are a variant of clustered entities. The structure of an organization is usually set up in many a styles, dependent on their objectives and ambience.
Strategic business unit	Strategic business unit or Strategic business unit is understood as a business unit within the overall corporate identity which is distinguishable from other business because it serves a defined external market where management can conduct strategic planning in relation to products and markets. When companies become really large, they are best thought of as being composed of a number of businesses (or Strategic business unit s.)
	In the broader domain of strategic management, the phrase Strategic business unit came into use in the 1960s, largely as a result of General Electric's many units.
Corporate culture	Organizational culture is not the same as corporate Culture. It is wider and deeper concepts, something that an organization 'is' rather than what it 'has' (according to Buchanan and Huczynski.)
	corporate Culture is the total sum of the values, customs, traditions and meanings that make a company unique.
Market	A market is any one of a variety of different systems, institutions, procedures, social relations and infrastructures whereby persons trade, and goods and services are exchanged, forming part of the economy. It is an arrangement that allows buyers and sellers to exchange things. market s vary in size, range, geographic scale, location, types and variety of human communities, as well as the types of goods and services traded.
Positioning	In marketing, positioning has come to mean the process by which marketers try to create an image or identity in the minds of their target market for its product, brand, or organization. It is the 'relative competitive comparison' their product occupies in a given market as perceived by the target market.

Chapter 5. Internal Scanning: Organizational Analysis

Chapter 5. Internal Scanning: Organizational Analysis

	Re-positioning involves changing the identity of a product, relative to the identity of competing products, in the collective minds of the target market.
Market segment	A market segment is a group of people or organizations sharing one or more characteristics that cause them to have similar product and/or service needs. A true market segment meets all of the following criteria: it is distinct from other segments (different segments have different needs), it is homogeneous within the segment (exhibits common needs); it responds similarly to a market stimulus, and it can be reached by a market intervention. The term is also used when consumers with identical product and/or service needs are divided up into groups so they can be charged different amounts.
Marketing	Marketing is an integrated communications-based process through which individuals and communities discover that existing and newly-identified needs and wants may be satisfied by the products and services of others.
	Marketing is defined by the American Marketing Association as the activity, set of institutions, and processes for creating, communicating, delivering, and exchanging offerings that have value for customers, clients, partners, and society at large. The term developed from the original meaning which referred literally to going to market, as in shopping, or going to a market to buy or sell goods or services.
Marketing mix	The Marketing mix is generally accepted as the use and specification of the 'four P's' describing the strategic position of a product in the marketplace. One version of the Marketing mix originated in 1948 when James Culliton said that a marketing decision should be a result of something similar to a recipe. This version was used in 1953 when Neil Borden, in his American Marketing Association presidential address, took the recipe idea one step further and coined the term 'marketing-mix'.
Brand	A Brand is a name or trademark connected with a product or producer. Brand s have become increasingly important components of culture and the economy, now being described as 'cultural accessories and personal philosophies'.
	Some people distinguish the psychological aspect of a Brand from the experiential aspect.
Product life cycle	Product life cycle Management is the succession of strategies used by management as a product goes through its Product life cycle. The conditions in which a product is sold changes over time and must be managed as it moves through its succession of stages.
	The Product life cycle goes through many phases, involves many professional disciplines, and requires many skills, tools and processes.
Capital budgeting	Capital budgeting is the planning process used to determine whether a firm's long term investments such as new machinery, replacement machinery, new plants, new products, and research development projects are worth pursuing. It is budget for major capital, or investment, expenditures.
	Many formal methods are used in Capital budgeting, including the techniques such as · Net present value · Profitability index · Internal rate of return · Modified Internal Rate of Return · Equivalent annuity

Chapter 5. Internal Scanning: Organizational Analysis

	These methods use the incremental cash flows from each potential investment, or project. Techniques based on accounting earnings and accounting rules are sometimes used - though economists consider this to be improper - such as the accounting rate of return, and 'return on investment.' Simplified and hybrid methods are used as well, such as payback period and discounted payback period.
Technology transfer	Technology transfer is the process of sharing of skills, knowledge, technologies, methods of manufacturing, samples of manufacturing and facilities among governments and other institutions to ensure that scientific and technological developments are accessible to a wider range of users who can then further develop and exploit the technology into new products, processes, applications, materials or services. It is closely related to (and may arguably be considered a subset of) Knowledge transfer. Related terms, used almost synonymously, include 'technology valorisation' and 'technology commercialisation'.
Continuous	In probability theory, a probability distribution is called continuous if its cumulative distribution function is continuous. This is equivalent to saying that for random variables X with the distribution in question, Pr[X = a] = 0 for all real numbers a, i.e.: the probability that X attains the value a is zero, for any number a. If the distribution of X is continuous then X is called a continuous random variable.
Experience curve	Models of the learning curve effect and the closely related Experience curve effect express the relationship between equations for experience and efficiency or between efficiency gains and investment in the effort. The experience of 'learning curves' was first observed by the 19th Century German psychologist Hermann Ebbinghaus according to the difficulty of memorizing varying numbers of verbal stimuli, and subsequent learning about the complex processes of learning are discussed in the . The rule used for representing the learning curve effect states that the more times a task has been performed, the less time will be required on each subsequent iteration.
Operating leverage	The Operating leverage is a measure of how revenue growth translates into growth in operating income. It is a measure of leverage, and of how risky (volatile) a company's operating income is. There are various measures of Operating leverage, which can be interpreted analogously to financial leverage.
Economies of scale	Economies of scale, in microeconomics, are the cost advantages that a business obtains due to expansion. They are factors that cause a producer's average cost per unit to fall as scale is increased. Economies of scale is a long run concept and refers to reductions in unit cost as the size of a facility, or scale, increases.
Flexible manufacturing	A Flexible manufacturing system is a manufacturing system in which there is some amount of flexibility that allows the system to react in the case of changes, whether predicted or unpredicted. This flexibility is generally considered to fall into two categories, which both contain numerous subcategories. The first category, machine flexibility, covers the system's ability to be changed to produce new product types, and ability to change the order of operations executed on a part. The second category is called routing flexibility, which consists of the ability to use multiple machines to perform the same operation on a part, as well as the system's ability to absorb large-scale changes, such as in volume, capacity, or capability.

Chapter 5. Internal Scanning: Organizational Analysis

Chapter 5. Internal Scanning: Organizational Analysis

Mass customization	Mass customization, in marketing, manufacturing, call centres and management, is the use of flexible computer-aided manufacturing systems to produce custom output. Those systems combine the low unit costs of mass production processes with the flexibility of individual customization. 'Mass customization' is the new frontier in business competition for both manufacturing and service industries.
Concurrent engineering	Concurrent engineering is a work methodology based on the parallelization of tasks (ie. concurrently.) It refers to an approach used in product development in which functions of design engineering, manufacturing engineering and other functions are integrated to reduce the elapsed time required to bring a new product to the market.
Virtual team	A Virtual team -- also known as a geographically dispersed team -- is a group of individuals who work across time, space, and organizational boundaries with links strengthened by webs of communication technology. They have complementary skills and are committed to a common purpose, have interdependent performance goals, and share an approach to work for which they hold themselves mutually accountable. Geographically dispersed teams allow organizations to hire and retain the best people regardless of location.
Diversity	The 'business case for diversity', theorizes that in a global marketplace, a company that employs a diverse workforce (both men and women, people of many generations, people from ethnically and racially diverse backgrounds etc.) is better able to understand the demographics of the marketplace it serves and is thus better equipped to thrive in that marketplace than a company that has a more limited range of employee demographics. An additional corollary suggests that a company that supports the diversity of its workforce can also improve employee satisfaction, productivity and retention.
Extranet	An Extranet is a private network that uses Internet protocols, network connectivity, and possibly the public telecommunication system to securely share part of an organization's information or operations with suppliers, vendors, partners, customers or other businesses. An Extranet can be viewed as part of a company's intranet that is extended to users outside the company (e.g.: normally over the Internet.) It has also been described as a 'state of mind' in which the Internet is perceived as a way to do business with a preapproved set of other companies business-to-business (B2B), in isolation from all other Internet users.
Intranet	An Intranet is a private computer network that uses Internet technologies to securely share any part of an organization's information or operational systems with its employees. Sometimes the term refers only to the organization's internal website, but often it is a more extensive part of the organization's computer infrastructure and private websites are an important component and focal point of internal communication and collaboration. An Intranet is built from the same concepts and technologies used for the Internet, such as client-server computing and the Internet Protocol Suite (TCP/IP.)
Radio-frequency identification	Radio-frequency identification is the use of an object (typically referred to as an RFID tag) applied to or incorporated into a product, animal, or person for the purpose of identification and tracking using radio waves. Some tags can be read from several meters away and beyond the line of sight of the reader. Most RFID tags contain at least two parts.

Chapter 5. Internal Scanning: Organizational Analysis

Supply chain	A Supply chain is the system of organizations, people, technology, activities, information and resources involved in moving a product or service from supplier to customer. Supply chain activities transform natural resources, raw materials and components into a finished product that is delivered to the end customer. In sophisticated Supply chain systems, used products may re-enter the Supply chain at any point where residual value is recyclable.
Supply chain management	Supply chain management is the management of a network of interconnected businesses involved in the ultimate provision of product and service packages required by end customers (Harland, 1996.) Supply chain management spans all movement and storage of raw materials, work-in-process inventory, and finished goods from point of origin to point of consumption (supply chain.)
	The definition an American professional association put forward is that Supply chain management encompasses the planning and management of all activities involved in sourcing, procurement, conversion, and logistics management activities.
Audit	The general definition of an audit is an evaluation of a person, organization, system, process, project or product. audit s are performed to ascertain the validity and reliability of information; also to provide an assessment of a system's internal control. The goal of an audit is to express an opinion on the person / organization/system (etc) in question, under evaluation based on work done on a test basis.
Reverse logistics	Reverse logistics stands for all operations related to the reuse of products and materials. It is 'the process of planning, implementing, and controlling the efficient, cost effective flow of raw materials, in-process inventory, finished goods and related information from the point of consumption to the point of origin for the purpose of recapturing value or proper disposal. More precisely, Reverse logistics is the process of moving goods from their typical final destination for the purpose of capturing value, or proper disposal.

Chapter 5. Internal Scanning: Organizational Analysis

Chapter 6. Strategy Formulation: Situation Analysis and Business Strategy

SWOT analysis	SWOT analysis is a strategic planning method used to evaluate the Strengths, Weaknesses, Opportunities, and Threats involved in a project or in a business venture. It involves specifying the objective of the business venture or project and identifying the internal and external factors that are favorable and unfavorable to achieving that objective. The technique is credited to Albert Humphrey, who led a convention at Stanford University in the 1960s and 1970s using data from Fortune 500 companies.
Business	A Business is a legally recognized organization designed to provide goods and/or services to consumers. Business es are predominant in capitalist economies, most being privately owned and formed to earn profit that will increase the wealth of its owners and grow the Business itself. The owners and operators of a Business have as one of their main objectives the receipt or generation of a financial return in exchange for work and acceptance of risk.
Business strategy	Business strategy refers to the aggregated strategies of single business firm or a strategic business unit (SBU) in a diversified corporation. According to Michael Porter, a firm must formulate a Business strategy that incorporates either cost leadership, differentiation or focus in order to achieve a sustainable competitive advantage and long-term success in its chosen arenas or industries. Functional strategies include marketing strategies, new product development strategies, human resource strategies, financial strategies, legal strategies, supply-chain strategies, and information technology management strategies.
Cost	In economics, business, retail, and accounting, a Cost is the value of money that has been used up to produce something, and hence is not available for use anymore. In economics, a Cost is an alternative that is given up as a result of a decision. In business, the Cost may be one of acquisition, in which case the amount of money expended to acquire it is counted as Cost.
Cost leadership	Cost leadership is a concept developed by Michael Porter, used in business strategy. It describes a way to establish the competitive advantage. Cost leadership, in basic words, means the lowest cost of operation in the industry.
Risk	In decision theory and estimation theory, the risk of an estimator, $\hat{\theta}$, of an unknown parameter of the distribution, θ, is the expected value of the loss function $$R(\theta, \hat{\theta}) = \mathbb{E}_\theta L(\theta, \hat{\theta}) = \int L(\theta, \hat{\theta}) \, dP_\theta.$$ where dP_θ is a probability measure parametrized by θ. · For a scalar parameter θ and a quadratic loss function, $$L(\theta, \hat{\theta}) = (\theta - \hat{\theta})^2$$ the risk function becomes the mean squared error of the estimate, $$R(\theta, \hat{\theta}) = E_\theta (\theta - \hat{\theta})^2$$ · In density estimation, the unknown parameter is probability density itself. The loss function is typically chosen to be a norm in an appropriate function space. For example, for L^2 norm,

Chapter 6. Strategy Formulation: Situation Analysis and Business Strategy

Chapter 6. Strategy Formulation: Situation Analysis and Business Strategy

$$L(f, \hat{f}) = \|f - \hat{f}\|_2^2$$

the risk function becomes the mean integrated squared error

$$R(f, \hat{f}) = E\|f - \hat{f}\|^2$$

Hypercompetition	Often a characteristic of new markets and industries, Hypercompetition occurs when technologies or offerings are so new that standards and rules are in flux, resulting in competitive advantages that cannot be sustained. In response, companies must constantly compete in price or quality, or innovate in supply chain management, new value creation, or have enough financial capital to outlast other competitors.
First-mover advantage	First-mover advantage is the advantage gained by the initial occupant of a market segment. This advantage may stem from the fact that the first entrant can gain control of resources that followers may not be able to match. Sometimes the first mover is not able to capitalise on its advantage, leaving the opportunity for another firm to gain second-mover advantage.
Market	A market is any one of a variety of different systems, institutions, procedures, social relations and infrastructures whereby persons trade, and goods and services are exchanged, forming part of the economy. It is an arrangement that allows buyers and sellers to exchange things. market s vary in size, range, geographic scale, location, types and variety of human communities, as well as the types of goods and services traded.
Collusion	Collusion is an agreement, usually secretive, which occurs between two or more persons to deceive, mislead or to obtain an objective forbidden by law typically involving fraud or gaining an unfair advantage. It is an agreement among firms to divide the market, set prices kickbacks, or misrepresenting the independence of the relationship between the colluding parties.' All acts effected by Collusion are considered void.
Strategic alliance	A strategic Alliance is a formal relationship between two or more parties to pursue a set of agreed upon goals or to meet a critical business need while remaining independent organizations.
	Partners may provide the strategic Alliance with resources such as products, distribution channels, manufacturing capability, project funding, capital equipment, knowledge, expertise, or intellectual property. The alliance is a cooperation or collaboration which aims for a synergy where each partner hopes that the benefits from the alliance will be greater than those from individual efforts.
Joint venture	A Joint venture is an entity formed between two or more parties to undertake economic activity together. The parties agree to create a new entity by both contributing equity, and they then share in the revenues, expenses, and control of the enterprise. The venture can be for one specific project only, or a continuing business relationship such as the Fuji Xerox Joint venture.
Comparative advertising	Comparative advertising is an advertisement in which a particular product specifically mentions a competitor by name for the express purpose of showing why the competitor is inferior to the product naming it.

This should not be confused with parody advertisements, where a fictional product is being advertised for the purpose of poking fun at the particular advertisement, nor should it be confused with the use of a coined brand name for the purpose of comparing the product without actually naming an actual competitor. ('Wikipedia tastes better and is less filling than the Encyclopedia Galactica.')

In the 1980s, during what has been referred to as the cola wars, soft-drink manufacturer Pepsi ran a series of advertisements where people, caught on hidden camera, in a blind taste test, chose Pepsi over rival Coca-Cola.

Partnership | A Partnership is a type of business entity in which partners (owners) share with each other the profits or losses of the business. Partnership s are often favored over corporations for taxation purposes, as the Partnership structure does not generally incur a tax on profits before it is distributed to the partners (i.e. there is no dividend tax levied.) However, depending on the Partnership structure and the jurisdiction in which it operates, owners of a Partnership may be exposed to greater personal liability than they would as shareholders of a corporation.

Chapter 6. Strategy Formulation: Situation Analysis and Business Strategy

Chapter 7. Strategy Formulation: Corporate Strategy

Corporate strategy	Corporate strategy refers to the overarching strategy of the diversified firm. Such a Corporate strategy answers the questions of 'in which businesses should we be in?' and 'how does being in these business create synergy and/or add to the competitive advantage of the corporation as a whole?'
	Business strategy refers to the aggregated strategies of single business firm or a strategic business unit (SBU) in a diversified corporation. According to Michael Porter, a firm must formulate a business strategy that incorporates either cost leadership, differentiation or focus in order to achieve a sustainable competitive advantage and long-term success in its chosen arenas or industries.
Acquisition	The phrase mergers and acquisitions refers to the aspect of corporate strategy, corporate finance and management dealing with the buying, selling and combining of different companies that can aid, finance, or help a growing company in a given industry grow rapidly without having to create another business entity.
	An Acquisition, also known as a takeover or a buyout, is the buying of one company (the 'target') by another. An Acquisition may be friendly or hostile.
Takeovers	Takeovers in the UK (meaning acquisitions of public companies only) are governed by the City Code on Takeovers and Mergers, also known as the 'City Code' or 'Takeover Code'. The rules for a takeover, can be found what is primarily known as 'The Blue Book'. The Code used to be a non-statutory set of rules that was controlled by City institutions on a theoretically voluntary basis.
Vertical integration	In microeconomics and management, the term vertical integration describes a style of management control. Vertically integrated companies are united through a hierarchy with a common owner. Usually each member of the hierarchy produces a different product or (market-specific) service, and the products combine to satisfy a common need.
Transaction cost	In economics and related disciplines, a Transaction cost is a cost incurred in making an economic exchange (restated: the cost of participating in a market.) For example, most people, when buying or selling a stock, must pay a commission to their broker; that commission is a Transaction cost of doing the stock deal. Or consider buying a banana from a store; to purchase the banana, your costs will be not only the price of the banana itself, but also the energy and effort it requires to find out which of the various banana products you prefer, where to get them and at what price, the cost of traveling from your house to the store and back, the time waiting in line, and the effort of the paying itself; the costs above and beyond the cost of the banana are the Transaction cost s.
International trade	International trade is exchange of capital, goods, and services across international borders or territories. In most countries, it represents a significant share of gross domestic product (GDP.) While International trade has been present throughout much of history , its economic, social, and political importance has been on the rise in recent centuries.
Horizontal integration	In microeconomics and strategic management, the term Horizontal integration describes a type of ownership and control. It is a strategy used by a business or corporation that seeks to sell a type of product in numerous markets. Horizontal integration in marketing is much more common than vertical integration is in production.
Outsourcing	Outsourcing is subcontracting a process, such as product design or manufacturing, to a third-party company. The decision to outsource is often made in the interest of lowering cost or making better use of time and energy costs, redirecting or conserving energy directed at the competencies of a particular business, or to make more efficient use of land, labor, capital, (information) technology and resources. Outsourcing became part of the business lexicon during the 1980s.

Chapter 7. Strategy Formulation: Corporate Strategy

Option	In finance, an option is a contract between a buyer and a seller that gives the buyer the right--but not the obligation--to buy or to sell a particular asset (the underlying asset) at a later day at an agreed price. In return for granting the option, the seller collects a payment (the premium) from the buyer. A call option gives the buyer the right to buy the underlying asset; a put option gives the buyer of the option the right to sell the underlying asset.
Franchising	Franchising refers to the methods of practicing and using another person's business philosophy. The franchisor grants the independent operator the right to distribute its products, techniques, and trademarks for a percentage of gross monthly sales and a royalty fee. Various tangibles and intangibles such as national or international advertising, training, and other support services are commonly made available by the franchisor.
Joint venture	A Joint venture is an entity formed between two or more parties to undertake economic activity together. The parties agree to create a new entity by both contributing equity, and they then share in the revenues, expenses, and control of the enterprise. The venture can be for one specific project only, or a continuing business relationship such as the Fuji Xerox Joint venture.
Synergy	Synergy is the term used to describe a situation where different entities cooperate advantageously for a final outcome. Simply defined, it means that the whole is greater than the sum of the individual parts. Although the whole will be greater than each individual part, this is not the concept of Synergy.
Bankruptcy	Bankruptcy is a legally declared inability or impairment of ability of an individual or organization to pay its creditors. Creditors may file a Bankruptcy petition against a debtor ('involuntary Bankruptcy') in an effort to recoup a portion of what they are owed or initiate a restructuring. In the majority of cases, however, Bankruptcy is initiated by the debtor (a 'voluntary Bankruptcy' that is filed by the insolvent individual or organization.)
Divestment	In finance and economics, Divestment or divestiture is the reduction of some kind of asset for either financial or ethical objectives or sale of an existing business by a firm. A Divestment is the opposite of an investment.
Liquidation	In law, liquidation refers to the process by which a company (or part of a company) is brought to an end, and the assets and property of the company redistributed. liquidation can also be referred to as winding-up or dissolution, although dissolution technically refers to the last stage of liquidation. The process of liquidation also arises when customs, an authority or agency in a country responsible for collecting and safeguarding customs duties, determines the final computation or ascertainment of the duties or drawback accruing on an entry.
Star	The STAR (Situation, Task, Action, Result) format is a job interview technique used by interviewers to gather all the relevant information about a specific capability that the job requires. This interview format is said to have a higher degree of predictability of future on-the-job performance than the traditional interview. · Situation: The interviewer wants you to present a recent challenge and situation in which you found yourself. · Task: What did you have to achieve? The interviewer will be looking to see what you were trying to achieve from the situation. · Action: What did you do? The interviewer will be looking for information on what you did, why you did it and what were the alternatives. · Results: What was the outcome of your actions? What did you achieve through your actions and did you meet your objectives. What did you learn from this experience and have you used this learning since? .

Chapter 7. Strategy Formulation: Corporate Strategy

Chapter 7. Strategy Formulation: Corporate Strategy

Business	A Business is a legally recognized organization designed to provide goods and/or services to consumers. Business es are predominant in capitalist economies, most being privately owned and formed to earn profit that will increase the wealth of its owners and grow the Business itself. The owners and operators of a Business have as one of their main objectives the receipt or generation of a financial return in exchange for work and acceptance of risk.
Strategic alliance	A strategic Alliance is a formal relationship between two or more parties to pursue a set of agreed upon goals or to meet a critical business need while remaining independent organizations.
	Partners may provide the strategic Alliance with resources such as products, distribution channels, manufacturing capability, project funding, capital equipment, knowledge, expertise, or intellectual property. The alliance is a cooperation or collaboration which aims for a synergy where each partner hopes that the benefits from the alliance will be greater than those from individual efforts.
Earnings per share	Earnings per share are the earnings returned on the initial investment amount.
	In the US, the Financial Accounting Standards Board (FASB) requires companies' income statements to report Earnings per share for each of the major categories of the income statement: continuing operations, discontinued operations, extraordinary items, and net income.
	The Earnings per share formula does not include preferred dividends for categories outside of continued operations and net income.

Chapter 8. Strategy Formulation: Functional Strategy and Strategic Choice

Market	A market is any one of a variety of different systems, institutions, procedures, social relations and infrastructures whereby persons trade, and goods and services are exchanged, forming part of the economy. It is an arrangement that allows buyers and sellers to exchange things. market s vary in size, range, geographic scale, location, types and variety of human communities, as well as the types of goods and services traded.
Market development	A Market development strategy targets non-buying customers in currently targeted segments. It also targets new customers in new segments. (Winer)
	A marketing manager has to think about the following questions before implementing a Market development strategy: Is it profitable? Will it require the introduction of new or modified products? Is the customer and channel well enough researched and understood?
	The marketing manager uses these four groups to give more focus to the market segment decision: existing customers, competitor customers, non-buying in current segments, new segments.
Marketing	Marketing is an integrated communications-based process through which individuals and communities discover that existing and newly-identified needs and wants may be satisfied by the products and services of others.
	Marketing is defined by the American Marketing Association as the activity, set of institutions, and processes for creating, communicating, delivering, and exchanging offerings that have value for customers, clients, partners, and society at large. The term developed from the original meaning which referred literally to going to market, as in shopping, or going to a market to buy or sell goods or services.
Marketing strategy	A marketing strategy is a process that can allow an organization to concentrate its limited resources on the greatest opportunities to increase sales and achieve a sustainable competitive advantage. A marketing strategy should be centered around the key concept that customer satisfaction is the main goal.
	A marketing strategy is a written plan which combines product development, promotion, distribution, and pricing approach, identifies the firm's marketing goals, and explains how they will be achieved within a stated timeframe.
Product development	In business and engineering, new Product development (N Product development) is the term used to describe the complete process of bringing a new product or service to market. There are two parallel paths involved in the N Product development process: one involves the idea generation, product design, and detail engineering; the other involves market research and marketing analysis. Companies typically see new Product development as the first stage in generating and commercializing new products within the overall strategic process of product life cycle management used to maintain or grow their market share.
Dynamic pricing	Why do retail stores need Dynamic pricing? With respect to the key objectives of growth and profit for any retail entity, Dynamic pricing should significantly improve sales margins and increase sales by enabling the vendor to price variably and hence suitably and to control its product range based on profit margins. The retail stores will be able to compete more effectively with rivals in the form of mixed multiples, mail order and online retailers, who are often able to undercut but who do not generally have the same understanding of the retail market. In particular Dynamic pricing is recognised as encouraging impulse buys, cross-selling of products and repeat sales.
Penetration pricing	Penetration pricing is the pricing technique of setting a relatively low initial entry price, often lower than the eventual market price, to attract new customers. The strategy works on the expectation that customers will switch to the new brand because of the lower price. Penetration pricing is most commonly associated with a marketing objective of increasing market share or sales volume, rather than to make profit in the short term.

Chapter 8. Strategy Formulation: Functional Strategy and Strategic Choice

Chapter 8. Strategy Formulation: Functional Strategy and Strategic Choice

Pricing	Pricing is one of the four Ps of the marketing mix. The other three aspects are product, promotion, and place. It is also a key variable in microeconomic price allocation theory.
Leveraged buyout	A Leveraged buyout (or Leveraged buyout O or 'bootstrap' transaction) occurs when a financial sponsor acquires a controlling interest in a company's equity and where a significant percentage of the purchase price is financed through leverage (borrowing.) The assets of the acquired company are used as collateral for the borrowed capital, sometimes with assets of the acquiring company. The bonds or other paper issued for Leveraged buyout s are commonly considered not to be investment grade because of the significant risks involved.
Open innovation	Open Innovation is a term promoted by Henry Chesbrough, a professor and executive director at the Center for open Innovation at Berkeley, in his book open Innovation: The new imperative for creating and profiting from technology. The concept is related to user innovation, cumulative innovation and distributed innovation.
	'open Innovation is a paradigm that assumes that firms can and should use external ideas as well as internal ideas, and internal and external paths to market, as the firms look to advance their technology'.
Flexible manufacturing	A Flexible manufacturing system is a manufacturing system in which there is some amount of flexibility that allows the system to react in the case of changes, whether predicted or unpredicted. This flexibility is generally considered to fall into two categories, which both contain numerous subcategories.
	The first category, machine flexibility, covers the system's ability to be changed to produce new product types, and ability to change the order of operations executed on a part. The second category is called routing flexibility, which consists of the ability to use multiple machines to perform the same operation on a part, as well as the system's ability to absorb large-scale changes, such as in volume, capacity, or capability.
Mass production	Mass production is the production of large amounts of standardized products, including and especially on assembly lines. The concepts of Mass production are applied to various kinds of products, from fluids and particulates handled in bulk to discrete solid parts to assemblies of such parts
	Mass production of assemblies typically uses electric-motor-powered moving tracks or conveyor belts to move partially complete products to workers, who perform simple repetitive tasks.
Continuous	In probability theory, a probability distribution is called continuous if its cumulative distribution function is continuous. This is equivalent to saying that for random variables X with the distribution in question, $Pr[X = a] = 0$ for all real numbers a, i.e.: the probability that X attains the value a is zero, for any number a. If the distribution of X is continuous then X is called a continuous random variable.
Continuous Improvement Process	Continuous Improvement Process is a management process whereby delivery (customer valued) processes are constantly evaluated and improved in the light of their efficiency, effectiveness and flexibility.
	Some see it as a meta process for most management systems (Business Process Management, Quality Management, Project Management). Deming saw it as part of the 'system' whereby feedback from the process and customer were evaluated against organisational goals.

Chapter 8. Strategy Formulation: Functional Strategy and Strategic Choice

Just-In-Time	Just-in-time is an inventory strategy that strives to improve the return on investment of a business by reducing in-process inventory and its associated carrying costs. To meet Just-in-time objectives, the process relies on signals between different points in the process. This means the process is often driven by a series of signals, or Kanban, which tell production when to make the next part. Kanban are usually 'tickets' but can be simple visual signals, such as the presence or absence of a part on a shelf. Implemented correctly, Just-in-time can dramatically improve a manufacturing organization's return on investment, quality, and efficiency.
Mass customization	Mass customization, in marketing, manufacturing, call centres and management, is the use of flexible computer-aided manufacturing systems to produce custom output. Those systems combine the low unit costs of mass production processes with the flexibility of individual customization. 'Mass customization' is the new frontier in business competition for both manufacturing and service industries.
No-bid contract	No-bid contract is a popular term for what is officially known as a 'sole source contract.' A sole source contract implies that there is only one person or company that can provide the contractual services needed and that any attempt to obtain bids would only result in one person or company being available to meet the need. It is awarded usually, but not always, by a government after soliciting and negotiating with only one firm These contracts can be negotiated much more quickly than a typical competitive contract but they are often fraught with suspicion that the company used illegal or immoral means to exclude competitors (usually cronyism or bribery).
Human Resource Management	Human resource management is the strategic and coherent approach to the management of an organisation's most valued assets - the people working there who individually and collectively contribute to the achievement of the objectives of the business. The terms 'Human resource management' and 'human resources' (HR) have largely replaced the term 'personnel management' as a description of the processes involved in managing people in organizations. In simple sense, Human resource management means employing people, developing their resources, utilizing, maintaining and compensating their services in tune with the job and organizational requirement.
Logistics	Logistics is the management of the flow of goods, information and other resources, including energy and people, between the point of origin and the point of consumption in order to meet the requirements of consumers (frequently, and originally, military organizations.) Logistics involves the integration of information, transportation, inventory, warehousing, material-handling, and packaging, and occasionally security. Logistics is a channel of the supply chain which adds the value of time and place utility.
Workforce	The workforce is the labour pool in employment. It is generally used to describe those working for a single company or industry, but can also apply to a geographic region like a city, country, state, etc. The term generally excludes the employers or management, and implies those involved in manual labour.
Outsourcing	Outsourcing is subcontracting a process, such as product design or manufacturing, to a third-party company. The decision to outsource is often made in the interest of lowering cost or making better use of time and energy costs, redirecting or conserving energy directed at the competencies of a particular business, or to make more efficient use of land, labor, capital, (information) technology and resources. Outsourcing became part of the business lexicon during the 1980s.
Sourcing	In business, the term word Sourcing refers to a number of procurement practices, aimed at finding, evaluating and engaging suppliers of goods and services:

Chapter 8. Strategy Formulation: Functional Strategy and Strategic Choice

Chapter 8. Strategy Formulation: Functional Strategy and Strategic Choice

· Global Sourcing a procurement strategy aimed at exploiting global efficiencies in production
· Strategic Sourcing a component of supply chain management, for improving and re-evaluating purchasing activities
- · Co Sourcing a type of auditing service
· Low-cost country Sourcing a procurement strategy for acquiring materials from countries with lower labour and production costs in order to cut operating expenses
· Corporate Sourcing a supply chain, purchasing/procurement, and inventory function
· Second-tier Sourcing a practice of rewarding suppliers for attempting to achieve minority-owned business spending goals of their customer
· Net Sourcing , a practice of utilizing an established group of businesses, individuals, or hardware ' software applications to streamline or initiate procurement practices by tapping in to and working through a third party provider
· Inverted Sourcing a price volatility reduction strategy usually conducted by procurement or supply-chain person by which the value of an organization's waste-stream is maximized by actively seeking out the highest price possible from a range of potential buyers exploiting price trends and other market factors
· Multi Sourcing , a strategy that treats a given function, such as IT, as a portfolio of activities, some of which should be outsourced and others of which should be performed by internal staff.
· Crowd Sourcing , using an undefined, generally large group of people or community in the form of an open call to perform a task

In journalism, it can also refer to:

· Journalism Sourcing the practice of identifying a person or publication that gives information
· Single Sourcing the reuse of content in publishing

In computing, it can refer to:

· Open Sourcing the act of releasing previously proprietary software under an open source/free software license
· Power Sourcing equipment, network devices that will provide power in a Power over Ethernet (PoE) setup .

Offshoring

Offshoring describes the relocation by a company of a business process from one country to another -- typically an operational process, such as manufacturing such as accounting. Even state governments employ Offshoring.

The term is in use in several distinct but closely related ways.

Risk

In decision theory and estimation theory, the risk of an estimator, $\hat{\theta}$, of an unknown parameter of the distribution, θ, is the expected value of the loss function

$$R(\theta, \hat{\theta}) = \mathbb{E}_\theta L(\theta, \hat{\theta}) = \int L(\theta, \hat{\theta}) \, dP_\theta.$$

where dP_θ is a probability measure parametrized by θ.

· For a scalar parameter θ and a quadratic loss function,

Chapter 8. Strategy Formulation: Functional Strategy and Strategic Choice

Chapter 8. Strategy Formulation: Functional Strategy and Strategic Choice

$$L(\theta, \hat{\theta}) = (\theta - \hat{\theta})^2$$

the risk function becomes the mean squared error of the estimate,

$$R(\theta, \hat{\theta}) = E_\theta(\theta - \hat{\theta})^2$$

· In density estimation, the unknown parameter is probability density itself. The loss function is typically chosen to be a norm in an appropriate function space. For example, for L^2 norm,

$$L(f, \hat{f}) = \|f - \hat{f}\|_2^2$$

the risk function becomes the mean integrated squared error

$$R(f, \hat{f}) = E\|f - \hat{f}\|^2$$

Net present value	Net present value or net present worth (NPW) is defined as the total present value (PV) of a time series of cash flows. It is a standard method for using the time value of money to appraise long-term projects. Used for capital budgeting, and widely throughout economics, it measures the excess or shortfall of cash flows, in present value terms, once financing charges are met.
Corporate culture	Organizational culture is not the same as corporate Culture. It is wider and deeper concepts, something that an organization 'is' rather than what it 'has' (according to Buchanan and Huczynski.)
	corporate Culture is the total sum of the values, customs, traditions and meanings that make a company unique.
Choice	Choice consists of the mental process of thinking involved with the process of judging the merits of multiple options and selecting one of them for action. Some simple examples include deciding whether to get up in the morning or go back to sleep, or selecting a given route for a journey. More complex examples (often decisions that affect what a person thinks or their core beliefs) include choosing a lifestyle, religious affiliation, or political position.

Chapter 8. Strategy Formulation: Functional Strategy and Strategic Choice

Chapter 9. Strategy Implementation: Organizing for Action

Six Sigma	Six Sigma is a business management strategy, initially implemented by Motorola, that today enjoys widespread application in many sectors of industry. Six Sigma seeks to improve the quality of process outputs by identifying and removing the causes of defects (errors) and variation in manufacturing and business processes. It uses a set of quality management methods, including statistical methods, and creates a special infrastructure of people within the organization ('Black Belts' etc.)
Budget	Budget generally refers to a list of all planned expenses and revenues. It is a plan for saving and spending. A Budget is an important concept in microeconomics, which uses a Budget line to illustrate the trade-offs between two or more goods.
Standard Operating Procedure	A Standard operating procedure is a set of instructions having the force of a directive, covering those features of operations that lend themselves to a definite or standardized procedure without loss of effectiveness. Standard Operating Policies and Procedures can be effective catalysts to drive performance improvement and improving organizational results.
Comparative advertising	Comparative advertising is an advertisement in which a particular product specifically mentions a competitor by name for the express purpose of showing why the competitor is inferior to the product naming it. This should not be confused with parody advertisements, where a fictional product is being advertised for the purpose of poking fun at the particular advertisement, nor should it be confused with the use of a coined brand name for the purpose of comparing the product without actually naming an actual competitor. ('Wikipedia tastes better and is less filling than the Encyclopedia Galactica.') In the 1980s, during what has been referred to as the cola wars, soft-drink manufacturer Pepsi ran a series of advertisements where people, caught on hidden camera, in a blind taste test, chose Pepsi over rival Coca-Cola.
Synergy	Synergy is the term used to describe a situation where different entities cooperate advantageously for a final outcome. Simply defined, it means that the whole is greater than the sum of the individual parts. Although the whole will be greater than each individual part, this is not the concept of Synergy.
Structure follows strategy	The historian Alfred Chandler substantiated his 'Structure follows strategy' thesis based on four case studies of American conglomerates that dominated their industry from the 1920s onward. Chandler described how the chemical company Du Pont, the automobile manufacturer General Motors, the energy company Standard Oil of New Jersey and the retailer Sears Roebuck managed a growth and diversification strategy by adopting the revolutionary multi-division form. The M-Form is a corporate federation of semi-independent product or geographic groups plus a headquarters that oversees the corporate strategy and coordinates interdependencies.
Leadership	Leadership has been described as the 'process of social influence in which one person can enlist the aid and support of others in the accomplishment of a common task'. A definition more inclusive of followers comes from Alan Keith of Genentech who said 'leadership is ultimately about creating a way for people to contribute to making something extraordinary happen.' leadership is one of the most salient aspects of the organizational context. However, defining leadership has been challenging.

Chapter 9. Strategy Implementation: Organizing for Action

Control	Control is one of the managerial functions like planning, organizing, staffing and directing. It is an important function because it helps to check the errors and to take the corrective action so that deviation from standards are minimized and stated goals of the organization are achieved in desired manner. According to modern concepts, Control is a foreseeing action whereas earlier concept of Control was used only when errors were detected. Control in management means setting standards, measuring actual performance and taking corrective action.
Organizational life cycle	Organizational life cycle is the life cycle of an organization from birth level to the termination. There are five level/stages in any organization. · Birth · Growth · Maturity · Decline · Death According to Richard L. Daft there are four stages in an Organizational life cycle. The four stages are: · Entrepreneurial stage -> Crisis: Need for leadership · Collectivity stage -> Crisis: Need for delegation · Formalization stage -> Crisis: Too much red tape · Elaboration stage -> Crisis: Need for revitalization (Richard L. Daft, Understanding the Theory and Design of Organizations, first edition 2007, ISBN 0-324-42271-7)
Organizational structure	An Organizational structure is a mostly hierarchical concept of subordination of entities that collaborate and contribute to serve one common aim. Organizations are a variant of clustered entities. The structure of an organization is usually set up in many a styles, dependent on their objectives and ambience.
Brand	A Brand is a name or trademark connected with a product or producer. Brand s have become increasingly important components of culture and the economy, now being described as 'cultural accessories and personal philosophies'. Some people distinguish the psychological aspect of a Brand from the experiential aspect.
Brand management	Brand management is the application of marketing techniques to a specific product, product line, or brand. It seeks to increase the product's perceived value to the customer and thereby increase brand franchise and brand equity. Marketers see a brand as an implied promise that the level of quality people have come to expect from a brand will continue with future purchases of the same product.
Work design	In organizational development (OD), work design is the application of Socio-Technical Systems principles and techniques to the humanization of work.

Chapter 9. Strategy Implementation: Organizing for Action

	The aims of work design to improved job satisfaction, to improved through-put, to improved quality and to reduced employee problems, e.g., grievances, absenteeism.
	Under scientific management people would be directed by reason and the problems of industrial unrest would be appropriately (i.e., scientifically) addressed.
Job enlargement	Job enlargement means increasing the scope of a job through extending the range of its job duties and responsibilities. This contradicts the principles of specialisation and the division of labour whereby work is divided into small units, each of which is performed repetitively by an individual worker. Some motivational theories suggest that the boredom and alienation caused by the division of labour can actually cause efficiency to fall.
Job enrichment	Job enrichment is an attempt to motivate employees by giving them the opportunity to use the range of their abilities. It is an idea that was developed by the American psychologist Frederick Herzberg in the 1950s. It can be contrasted to job enlargement which simply increases the number of tasks without changing the challenge.
Job rotation	Job rotation is an approach to management development where an individual is moved through a schedule of assignments designed to give him or her a breadth of exposure to the entire operation.
	job rotation is also practiced to allow qualified employees to gain more insights into the processes of a company, and to reduce boredom and increase job satisfaction through job variation.
	The term job rotation can also mean the scheduled exchange of persons in offices, especially in public offices, prior to the end of incumbency or the legislative period.
Multinational Corporation	A Multinational corporation or transnational corporation is a corporation or enterprise that manages production or delivers services in more than one country. It can also be referred to as an international corporation.
	The first modern Multinational corporation is generally thought to be the Dutch East India Company, established in 1602.
Strategic alliance	A strategic Alliance is a formal relationship between two or more parties to pursue a set of agreed upon goals or to meet a critical business need while remaining independent organizations.
	Partners may provide the strategic Alliance with resources such as products, distribution channels, manufacturing capability, project funding, capital equipment, knowledge, expertise, or intellectual property. The alliance is a cooperation or collaboration which aims for a synergy where each partner hopes that the benefits from the alliance will be greater than those from individual efforts.
Centralization	Centralization is the process by which the activities of an organisation, particularly those regarding decision-making, become concentrated within a particular location and/or group.
Decentralization	Decentralization is the process of dispersing decision-making governance closer to the people or citizen. It includes the dispersal of administration or governance in sectors or areas like engineering, management science, political science, political economy, sociology and economics. Decentralization is also possible in the dispersal of population and employment.

Chapter 9. Strategy Implementation: Organizing for Action

Chapter 9. Strategy Implementation: Organizing for Action

Game	A Game is a structured activity, usually undertaken for enjoyment and sometimes used as an educational tool. Game s are distinct from work, which is usually carried out for remuneration, and from art, which is more concerned with the expression of ideas. However, the distinction is not clear-cut, and many Game s are also considered to be work (such as professional players of spectator sports/ Game s) or art (such as jigsaw puzzles or Game s involving an artistic layout such as Mah-jongg solitaire.)

Chapter 10. Strategy Implementation: Staffing and Directing

Portfolio manager	A Portfolio manager is a person who makes investment decisions using money other people have placed under his or her control. In other words, it is a financial career involved in investment management. They work with a team of analysts and researchers, and are ultimately responsible for establishing an investment strategy, selecting appropriate investments and allocating each investment properly for a fund- or asset-management vehicle.
Job rotation	Job rotation is an approach to management development where an individual is moved through a schedule of assignments designed to give him or her a breadth of exposure to the entire operation.
job rotation is also practiced to allow qualified employees to gain more insights into the processes of a company, and to reduce boredom and increase job satisfaction through job variation.
The term job rotation can also mean the scheduled exchange of persons in offices, especially in public offices, prior to the end of incumbency or the legislative period.
Performance appraisal	Performance appraisal is a method by which the job performance of an employee is evaluated Performance appraisal is a part of career development.
Performance appraisal s are regular reviews of employee performance within organizations
Generally, the aims of a Performance appraisal are to:

· Give feedback on performance to employees.
· Identify employee training needs.
· Document criteria used to allocate organizational rewards.
· Form a basis for personnel decisions: salary increases, promotions, disciplinary actions, etc.
· Provide the opportunity for organizational diagnosis and development.
· Facilitate communication between employee and administraton
· Validate selection techniques and human resource policies to meet federal Equal Employment Opportunity requirements.
A common approach to assessing performance is to use a numerical or scalar rating system whereby managers are asked to score an individual against a number of objectives/attributes. In some companies, employees receive assessments from their manager, peers, subordinates and customers while also performing a self assessment. |
| Expatriate | An Expatriate is a person temporarily or permanently residing in a country and culture other than that of the person's upbringing or legal residence. The word comes from the Latin ex and patria (country, fatherland.)
The term is sometimes used in the context of Westerners living in non-Western countries, although it is also used to describe Westerners living in other Western countries, such as Americans living in the United Kingdom, or Britons living in Spain. |
| Corporate culture | Organizational culture is not the same as corporate Culture. It is wider and deeper concepts, something that an organization 'is' rather than what it 'has' (according to Buchanan and Huczynski.)
corporate Culture is the total sum of the values, customs, traditions and meanings that make a company unique. |
| Continuous | In probability theory, a probability distribution is called continuous if its cumulative distribution function is continuous. This is equivalent to saying that for random variables X with the distribution in question, $Pr[X = a] = 0$ for all real numbers a, i.e.: the probability that X attains the value a is zero, for any number a. If the distribution of X is continuous then X is called a continuous random variable. |

Chapter 10. Strategy Implementation: Staffing and Directing

Chapter 10. Strategy Implementation: Staffing and Directing

Continuous Improvement Process	Continuous Improvement Process is a management process whereby delivery (customer valued) processes are constantly evaluated and improved in the light of their efficiency, effectiveness and flexibility.
	Some see it as a meta process for most management systems (Business Process Management, Quality Management, Project Management). Deming saw it as part of the 'system' whereby feedback from the process and customer were evaluated against organisational goals.
Customer	A Customer also client, buyer or purchaser is usually used to refer to a current or potential buyer or user of the products of an individual or organization, mostly called the supplier or seller. This is typically through purchasing or renting goods or services. However in certain contexts the term Customer also includes by extension anyone who uses or experiences the services of another.
Customer satisfaction	Customer satisfaction, a business term, is a measure of how products and services supplied by a company meet or surpass customer expectation. It is seen as a key performance indicator within business and is part of the four perspectives of a Balanced Scorecard.
	In a competitive marketplace where businesses compete for customers, Customer satisfaction is seen as a key differentiator and increasingly has become a key element of business strategy.
Management By Objectives	Management by objectives is a process of agreeing upon objectives within an organization so that management and employees agree to the objectives and understand what they are in the organization.
	The term 'Management by objectives' was first popularized by Peter Drucker in his 1954 book 'The Practice of Management'.
	The essence of Management by objectives is participative goal setting, choosing course of actions and decision making.
Quality Management	Quality management can be considered to have three main components: quality control, quality assurance and quality improvement. Quality management is focused not only on product quality, but also the means to achieve it. Quality management therefore uses quality assurance and control of processes as well as products to achieve more consistent quality.
Total Quality Management	Total Quality Management is a business management strategy aimed at embedding awareness of quality in all organizational processes. Total Quality Management has been widely used in manufacturing, education, hospitals, call centers, government, and service industries, as well as NASA space and science programs.
	As defined by the International Organization for Standardization (ISO):
	'Total Quality Management is a management approach for an organization, centered on quality, based on the participation of all its members and aiming at long-term success through customer satisfaction, and benefits to all members of the organization and to society.' ISO 8402:1994
	One major aim is to reduce variation from every process so that greater consistency of effort is obtained. (Royse, D., Thyer, B., Padgett D., ' Logan T., 2006)

Chapter 10. Strategy Implementation: Staffing and Directing

Chapter 10. Strategy Implementation: Staffing and Directing

Quality circle	A Quality circle is a volunteer group composed of workers (or even students), usually under the leadership of their supervisor (but they can elect a team leader), who are trained to identify, analyse and solve work-related problems and present their solutions to management in order to improve the performance of the organization, and motivate and enrich the work of employees. When matured, true Quality circle s become self-managing, having gained the confidence of management. Quality circle s are an alternative to the dehumanising concept of the Division of Labour, where workers or individuals are treated like robots.
Control	Control is one of the managerial functions like planning, organizing, staffing and directing. It is an important function because it helps to check the errors and to take the corrective action so that deviation from standards are minimized and stated goals of the organization are achieved in desired manner. According to modern concepts, Control is a foreseeing action whereas earlier concept of Control was used only when errors were detected. Control in management means setting standards, measuring actual performance and taking corrective action.
Star	The STAR (Situation, Task, Action, Result) format is a job interview technique used by interviewers to gather all the relevant information about a specific capability that the job requires. This interview format is said to have a higher degree of predictability of future on-the-job performance than the traditional interview. · Situation: The interviewer wants you to present a recent challenge and situation in which you found yourself. · Task: What did you have to achieve? The interviewer will be looking to see what you were trying to achieve from the situation. · Action: What did you do? The interviewer will be looking for information on what you did, why you did it and what were the alternatives. · Results: What was the outcome of your actions? What did you achieve through your actions and did you meet your objectives. What did you learn from this experience and have you used this learning since? .
Keirsey Temperament Sorter	The Keirsey Temperament Sorter is a self-assessed personality questionnaire designed to help people better understand themselves and others. It was first introduced in the book Please Understand Me. The Keirsey Temperament Sorter is closely associated with the Myers-Briggs Type Indicator (MBTI); however, there are significant practical and theoretical differences between the two personality questionnaires and their associated different descriptions.

Chapter 10. Strategy Implementation: Staffing and Directing

Chapter 11. Evaluation and Control

Control	Control is one of the managerial functions like planning, organizing, staffing and directing. It is an important function because it helps to check the errors and to take the corrective action so that deviation from standards are minimized and stated goals of the organization are achieved in desired manner. According to modern concepts, Control is a foreseeing action whereas earlier concept of Control was used only when errors were detected. Control in management means setting standards, measuring actual performance and taking corrective action.
Earnings per share	Earnings per share are the earnings returned on the initial investment amount. In the US, the Financial Accounting Standards Board (FASB) requires companies' income statements to report Earnings per share for each of the major categories of the income statement: continuing operations, discontinued operations, extraordinary items, and net income. The Earnings per share formula does not include preferred dividends for categories outside of continued operations and net income.
Inventory turnover	The Inventory turnover is an equation that equals the cost of goods sold divided by the average inventory. Average inventory equals beginning inventory plus ending inventory divided by 2. The formula for Inventory turnover: The formula for average inventory: A low turnover rate may point to overstocking, obsolescence, or deficiencies in the product line or marketing effort.
Inventory turnover ratio	Inventory turnover ratio is one of the Accounting Liquidity ratios, a financial ratio. This ratio measures the number of times, on average, the inventory is sold during the period. Its purpose is to measure the liquidity of the inventory.
Activity-based costing	Activity-based costing is a costing model that identifies activities in an organization and assigns the cost of each activity resource to all products and services according to the actual consumption by each: it assigns more indirect costs (overhead) into direct costs. In this way an organization can establish the true cost of its individual products and services for the purposes of identifying and eliminating those which are unprofitable and lowering the prices of those which are overpriced. In a business organization, the ABC methodology assigns an organization's resource costs through activities to the products and services provided to its customers.
Chief Risk Officer	The Chief risk officer or chief risk management officer (CRMO) of a corporation is the executive accountable for enabling the efficient and effective governance of significant risks, and related opportunities, to a business and its various segments. Risks are commonly categorized as strategic, reputational, operational, financial, or compliance-related. Chief risk officer's are accountable to the Executive Committee and The Board for enabling the business to balance risk and reward.

Chapter 11. Evaluation and Control

Chapter 11. Evaluation and Control

Enterprise Risk Management

Enterprise risk management in business includes the methods and processes used by organizations to manage risks and seize opportunities related to the achievement of their objectives. Enterprise risk management provides a framework for risk management, which typically involves identifying particular events or circumstances relevant to the organization's objectives (risks and opportunities), assessing them in terms of likelihood and magnitude of impact, determining a response strategy, and monitoring progress. By identifying and proactively addressing risks and opportunities, business enterprises protect and create value for their stakeholders, including owners, employees, customers, regulators, and society overall.

Risk

In decision theory and estimation theory, the risk of an estimator, $\hat{\theta}$, of an unknown parameter of the distribution, θ, is the expected value of the loss function

$$R(\theta, \hat{\theta}) = \mathbb{E}_\theta L(\theta, \hat{\theta}) = \int L(\theta, \hat{\theta}) \, dP_\theta.$$

where dP_θ is a probability measure parametrized by θ.

- For a scalar parameter θ and a quadratic loss function,

$$L(\theta, \hat{\theta}) = (\theta - \hat{\theta})^2$$

the risk function becomes the mean squared error of the estimate,

$$R(\theta, \hat{\theta}) = E_\theta (\theta - \hat{\theta})^2$$

- In density estimation, the unknown parameter is probability density itself. The loss function is typically chosen to be a norm in an appropriate function space. For example, for L^2 norm,

$$L(f, \hat{f}) = \|f - \hat{f}\|_2^2$$

the risk function becomes the mean integrated squared error

$$R(f, \hat{f}) = E\|f - \hat{f}\|^2$$

Scenario planning

Scenario planning is a strategic planning method that some organizations use to make flexible long-term plans. It is in large part an adaptation and generalization of classic methods used by military intelligence.

The original method was that a group of analysts would generate simulation games for policy makers. In business applications, the emphasis on gaming the behavior of opponents was reduced (shifting more toward a game against nature). At Royal Dutch/Shell for example, Scenario planning was viewed as changing mindsets about the exogenous part of the world, prior to formulating specific strategies.

Chapter 11. Evaluation and Control

Chapter 11. Evaluation and Control

Free cash flow	In corporate finance, Free cash flow is cash flow available for distribution among all the securities holders of an organization. They include equity holders, debt holders, preferred stock holders, convertible security holders, and so on. Note that the first three lines above are calculated for you on the standard Statement of Cash Flows.
Mind share	Mind share is one of the main objectives of advertising and promotion. When people think of examples of a product type or category, they usually think of a limited number of brand names. For example, a prospective buyer of a college education will have several thousand colleges to choose from.
Operating cash flow	In financial accounting, Operating cash flow , cash flow provided by operations or cash flow from operating activities, refers to the amount of cash a company generates from the revenues it brings in, excluding costs associated with long-term investment on capital items or investment in securities. To calculate cash generated from operations, one must calculate cash generated from customers and cash paid to suppliers.
Return On Equity	Return on equity(requity)measures the rate of return on the ownership interest (shareholders' equity) of the common stock owners. It measures a firm's efficiency at generating profits from every dollar of shareholders' equity (also known as net assets or assets minus liabilities.) It shows how well a company uses investment dollars to generate earnings growth.
Shareholder	A mutual Shareholder or stockholder is an individual or company (including a corporation) that legally owns one or more shares of stock in a joint stock company. A company's Shareholder s collectively own that company. Thus, the typical goal of such companies is to enhance Shareholder value.
Shareholder value	Shareholder value is a business buzz term, which implies that the ultimate measure of a company's success is to enrich shareholders. It became popular during the 1980s, and is particularly associated with former CEO of General Electric, Jack Welch. In March 2009, Welch openly turned his back on the concept, calling Shareholder value 'the dumbest idea in the world'.
Economic Value Added	In corporate finance, Economic value added or Economic value added is an estimate of true economic profit after making corrective adjustments to GAAP accounting, including deducting the opportunity cost of equity capital. Economic value added can be measured as Net Operating Profit After Taxes(or NOPAT) less the money cost of capital. Economic value added is similar in nature to that of calculating another financial performance measure - Residual Income , however, there are a few complexities involved with coming up with the elements for calculating Economic value added over RI such as the myriad adjustments that might be made to NOPAT before it is suitable for the formula below.
Market	A market is any one of a variety of different systems, institutions, procedures, social relations and infrastructures whereby persons trade, and goods and services are exchanged, forming part of the economy. It is an arrangement that allows buyers and sellers to exchange things. market s vary in size, range, geographic scale, location, types and variety of human communities, as well as the types of goods and services traded.
Market Value	Market value is the price at which an asset would trade in a competitive Walrasian auction setting. Market value is often used interchangeably with open Market value, fair value or fair Market value, although these terms have distinct definitions in different standards, and may differ in some circumstances.

Chapter 11. Evaluation and Control

Chapter 11. Evaluation and Control

	International Valuation Standards defines Market value as 'the estimated amount for which a property should exchange on the date of valuation between a willing buyer and a willing seller in an arm's-length transaction after proper marketing wherein the parties had each acted knowledgeably, prudently, and without compulsion.'
	Market value is a concept distinct from market price, which is 'the price at which one can transact', while Market value is 'the true underlying value' according to theoretical standards.
Market Value Added	Market value added is the difference between the current market value of a firm and the capital contributed by investors. If Market value added is positive, the firm has added value. If it is negative, the firm has destroyed value.
Value added	Value added refers to the difference between the cost of materials purchased by a company plus the cost of the labor to assemble a product and the price at which the company sells the product. An example is the price of gasoline at the pump over the price of the oil in it. In national accounts used in macroeconomics, it refers to the contribution of the factors of production, i.e., land, labor, and capital goods, to raising the value of a product and corresponds to the incomes received by the owners of these factors.
Balanced scorecard	The Balanced scorecard is a performance management tool for measuring whether the smaller-scale operational activities of a company are aligned with its larger-scale objectives in terms of vision and strategy.
	By focusing not only on financial outcomes but also on the operational, marketing and developmental inputs to these, the Balanced scorecard helps provide a more comprehensive view of a business, which in turn helps organizations act in their best long-term interests. This tool is also being used to address business response to climate change and greenhouse gas emissions.
Board of directors	A Board of directors is a body of elected or appointed members who jointly oversee the activities of a company or organization. The body sometimes has a different name, such as board of trustees, board of governors, board of managers, or executive board. It is often simply referred to as 'the board.'
	A board's activities are determined by the powers, duties, and responsibilities delegated to it or conferred on it by an authority outside itself.
Audit	The general definition of an audit is an evaluation of a person, organization, system, process, project or product. audit s are performed to ascertain the validity and reliability of information; also to provide an assessment of a system's internal control. The goal of an audit is to express an opinion on the person / organization/system (etc) in question, under evaluation based on work done on a test basis.
Operating budget	An Operating budget is the annual budget of an activity stated in terms of Budget Classification Code, functional/subfunctional categories and cost accounts. It contains estimates of the total value of resources required for the performance of the operation including reimbursable work or services for others. It also includes estimates of workload in terms of total work units identified by cost accounts.
Cost	In economics, business, retail, and accounting, a Cost is the value of money that has been used up to produce something, and hence is not available for use anymore. In economics, a Cost is an alternative that is given up as a result of a decision. In business, the Cost may be one of acquisition, in which case the amount of money expended to acquire it is counted as Cost.
Profit center	Profit center s are parts of a corporation that directly add to its profit.

Chapter 11. Evaluation and Control

Chapter 11. Evaluation and Control

	A Profit center manager is held accountable for both revenues, and costs (expenses), and therefore, profits. What this means in terms of managerial responsibilities is that the manager has to drive the sales revenue generating activities which leads to cash inflows and at the same time control the cost (cash outflows) causing activities.
Transfer pricing	Transfer pricing refers to the pricing of contributions (assets, tangible and intangible, services, and funds) transferred within an organization. For example, goods from the production division may be sold to the marketing division, or goods from a parent company may be sold to a foreign subsidiary. Since the prices are set within an organization (i.e. controlled), the typical market mechanisms that establish prices for such transactions between third parties may not apply.
Benchmarking	Benchmarking is the process of comparing the cost, cycle time, productivity, or quality of a specific process or method to another that is widely considered to be an industry standard or best practice. Essentially, Benchmarking provides a snapshot of the performance of your business and helps you understand where you are in relation to a particular standard. The result is often a business case for making changes in order to make improvements.
Budget	Budget generally refers to a list of all planned expenses and revenues. It is a plan for saving and spending. A Budget is an important concept in microeconomics, which uses a Budget line to illustrate the trade-offs between two or more goods.
Enterprise Resource Planning	Enterprise resource planning is a company-wide computer software system used to manage and coordinate all the resources, information, and functions of a business from shared data stores.
	An Enterprise resource planning system has a service-oriented architecture with modular hardware and software units and 'services' that communicate on a local area network. The modular design allows a business to add or reconfigure modules (perhaps from different vendors) while preserving data integrity in one shared database that may be centralized or distributed.
Strategic information system	A Strategic information system is a system to manage information and assist in strategic decision making. A Strategic information system has been defined as, 'The information system to support or change enterprise's strategy.'
	A Strategic information system is a type of Information System that is aligned with business strategy and structure. The alignment increases the capability to respond faster to environmental changes and thus creates a competitive advantage.
Radio-frequency identification	Radio-frequency identification is the use of an object (typically referred to as an RFID tag) applied to or incorporated into a product, animal, or person for the purpose of identification and tracking using radio waves. Some tags can be read from several meters away and beyond the line of sight of the reader.
	Most RFID tags contain at least two parts.
Goal	A Goal or objective is a projected state of affairs that a person or a system plans or intends to achieve--a personal or organizational desired end-point in some sort of assumed development. Many people endeavor to reach Goal s within a finite time by setting deadlines.
	A desire or an intention becomes a Goal if and only if one activates an action for achieving it

Chapter 11. Evaluation and Control

Chapter 11. Evaluation and Control

| Incentive | In economics and sociology, an incentive is any factor (financial or non-financial) that enables or motivates a particular course of action, or counts as a reason for preferring one choice to the alternatives. It is an expectation that encourages people to behave in a certain way. Since human beings are purposeful creatures, the study of incentive structures is central to the study of all economic activity (both in terms of individual decision-making and in terms of co-operation and competition within a larger institutional structure.) |

Chapter 11. Evaluation and Control

Chapter 12. Suggestions for Case Analysis

Annual report	An Annual report is a comprehensive report on a company's activities throughout the preceding year. Annual report s are intended to give shareholders and other interested persons information about the company's activities and financial performance. Most jurisdictions require companies to prepare and disclose Annual report s, and many require the Annual report to be filed at the company's registry.
Financial analysis	Financial analysis refers to an assessment of the viability, stability and profitability of a business, sub-business or project.
	It is performed by professionals who prepare reports using ratios that make use of information taken from financial statements and other reports. These reports are usually presented to top management as one of their bases in making business decisions.
Gearing	In finance, gearing is borrowing money to supplement existing funds for investment in such a way that the potential positive or negative outcome is magnified and/or enhanced. It generally refers to using borrowed funds, or debt, so as to attempt to increase the returns to equity. Deleveraging is the action of reducing borrowings.
Liquidity	Market Liquidity is a business, economics or investment term that refers to an asset's ability to be easily converted through an act of buying or selling without causing a significant movement in the price and with minimum loss of value. Money, or cash on hand, is the most liquid asset. An act of exchange of a less liquid asset with a more liquid asset is called liquidation.
Financial statements	Financial statements are formal records of the financial activities of a business, person, or other entity. In British English, including United Kingdom company law, Financial statements are often referred to as accounts, although the term Financial statements is also used, particularly by accountants.
	Financial statements provide an overview of a business or person's financial condition in both short and long term.
Bankruptcy	Bankruptcy is a legally declared inability or impairment of ability of an individual or organization to pay its creditors. Creditors may file a Bankruptcy petition against a debtor ('involuntary Bankruptcy') in an effort to recoup a portion of what they are owed or initiate a restructuring. In the majority of cases, however, Bankruptcy is initiated by the debtor (a 'voluntary Bankruptcy' that is filed by the insolvent individual or organization.)
Turnover	In a human resources context, turnover or labor turnover is the rate at which an employer gains and loses employees. Simple ways to describe it are 'how long employees tend to stay' or 'the rate of traffic through the revolving door.' turnover is measured for individual companies and for their industry as a whole. If an employer is said to have a high turnover relative to its competitors, it means that employees of that company have a shorter average tenure than those of other companies in the same industry.
Constant dollars	The term Constant dollars refers to a metric for valuing the price of something over time, without that metric changing due to inflation or deflation. The term specifically refers to dollars whose present value is linked to a given year.
	As an example, this is a graph of 2005 Constant dollars:
	Constant dollars are used to compare the 'real value' of an income or price to put the 'nominal value' in perspective.
Consumer	Consumer is a broad label that refers to any individuals or households that use goods and services generated within the economy. The concept of a Consumer is used in different contexts, so that the usage and significance of the term may vary.

Chapter 12. Suggestions for Case Analysis

Chapter 12. Suggestions for Case Analysis

	Typically when business people and economists talk of Consumer s they are talking about person as Consumer an aggregated commodity item with little individuality other than that expressed in the buy/not-buy decision.
Consumer Price Index	A Consumer price index is a measure of the average price of consumer goods and services purchased by households. A Consumer price index measures a price change for a constant market basket of goods and services from one period to the next within the same area (city, region, or nation.) It is a price index determined by measuring the price of a standard group of goods meant to represent the typical market basket of a typical urban consumer.
Prime rate	Prime rate is a term applied in many countries to a reference interest rate used by banks. The term originally indicated the rate of interest at which banks lent to favored customers, i.e., those with high credibility, though this is no longer always the case. Some variable interest rates may be expressed as a percentage above or below Prime rate.
Gross domestic product	The Gross domestic product or gross domestic income (GDI), a basic measure of an economy's economic performance, is the market value of all final goods and services made within the borders of a nation in a year. Gross domestic product can be defined in three ways, all of which are conceptually identical. First, it is equal to the total expenditures for all final goods and services produced within the country in a stipulated period of time (usually a 365-day year).
Audit	The general definition of an audit is an evaluation of a person, organization, system, process, project or product. audit s are performed to ascertain the validity and reliability of information; also to provide an assessment of a system's internal control. The goal of an audit is to express an opinion on the person / organization/system (etc) in question, under evaluation based on work done on a test basis.
Case analysis	Case analysis is one of the most general and applicable methods of analytical thinking, depending only on the division of a problem, decision or situation into a sufficient number of separate cases. Analysing each such case individually may be enough to resolve the initial question. The principle of Case analysis is invoked in the celebrated remark of Sherlock Holmes, to the effect that when one has eliminated the impossible, what remains must be true, however unlikely that seems.